CU00689656

Morocco Tourist Guide 2023.

The Ultimate Guide to discovering Morocco's Culture, Landscapes, and Cuisine with Insider Tips, Must-See Destinations and an itinerary Guide.

Sheila D. Kidd

All rights reserved. No part of this publication may be reproduced, distributed, or transmitted in any form or by any means, including photocopying, recording, or other electronic or mechanical methods, without the prior written permission of the publisher, except in the case of brief quotations embodied in critical reviews and certain other noncommercial uses permitted by copyright law.

Copyright @ Sheila D. Kidd, 2023.

Table of contents

Introduction

Welcome to the Morocco Vacation Guide 2023! We are happy to be your companion while you experience one of the most exciting and varied nations in the world.

Morocco is a country that awakens the imagination with its brilliant colors, great food, and magnificent scenery. From the busy streets of Marrakech to the meandering lanes of Fez, Morocco provides a multitude of experiences for every tourist. Whether you're seeking adventure, leisure, or cultural immersion, you're sure to find it in Morocco.

This handbook is intended to help you make the most of your vacation to Morocco. We have accumulated a plethora of information on the greatest locations to visit, the most delectable local food, and the most engaging cultural activities. We've also included practical tips on visas, transportation, and lodgings, so you can feel assured on your trips.

In these pages, you will discover the major attractions and hidden jewels of Morocco, from the breathtaking mountains of the Atlas range to the enormous expanse of the Sahara Desert. You'll also get exclusive insights and ideas from residents and seasoned tourists, to help you explore the nation like a real Moroccan.

We hope that this handbook will encourage you to discover the beauty of Morocco and create wonderful experiences that will last a lifetime. So get a book, pack your luggage, and get ready for an experience of a lifetime in Morocco!

Top Reasons to Visit Morocco

Morocco is a bustling nation situated in North Africa, and it provides a vast selection of activities that might appeal to a wide variety of people. Here are some top reasons to visit Morocco:

1. **Rich Culture:**

Morocco has a rich cultural past, inspired by Berber, Arab, and French colonial traditions. Visitors may experience this unique combination of cultures via music, cuisine, architecture, and art.

2. **Scenic Beauty:**

Morocco is home to beautiful scenery, including the Sahara desert, the High Atlas Mountains, and the Mediterranean and Atlantic beaches. The nation provides lots of options for hiking, skiing, surfing, and other outdoor activities.

3. Unique Architecture:

Morocco's architecture is remarkable, with its colorful tilework, elaborate woodcarvings, and elegant entrances. Visitors may visit ancient structures like the Kasbahs, medinas, and palaces, which display this particular design.

4. Delicious Cuisine:

Moroccan food is rich and diversified, with a variety of spices, meats, vegetables, and fruits. meals like tagine, couscous, and harira are popular mainstays, and tourists may enjoy a broad choice of street cuisine and traditional meals.

5. Warm Hospitality:

Moroccans are famed for their warm hospitality, and tourists can expect to be greeted with open arms. The nation is home to a dynamic population of residents and ex-pats, who are ready to share their culture and customs with tourists.

6. Shopping:

Morocco is a shopper's dream, with its busy marketplaces, or souks, providing a broad variety of items, including spices, textiles, jewelry, and pottery. Visitors may also peruse trendy boutiques and designer stores in locations like Marrakech and Casablanca.

7. Historical Sites:

Morocco is home to various old historical monuments, including the Roman remains of

Volubilis, the medieval city of Fes, and the Kasbah of Ait Ben Haddou. These locations look into Morocco's rich history and cultural heritage.

Overall, Morocco is a fascinating location that provides a unique combination of cultural, historical, and natural features, making it a great destination for tourists seeking a genuine and diversified experience.

Overview of Morocco

Morocco is located in North Africa and is bordered by the Atlantic Ocean to the west, the Mediterranean Sea to the north, Algeria to the east and southeast, and the disputed territory of the Western Sahara to the south. Spain controls two enclaves in northern Morocco and several islands offshore.

France ruled over most of Morocco as a protectorate from 1912 to 1956, while Spain governed the northern part of the country during the same period. A war between Spain and Morocco in 1860 established Spain's claim to a small area on the southern Atlantic coast of Morocco called Ifni.

The Treaty of Fes in 1912 gave Spain control over the district of Tarfaya near Western Sahara, but it was returned to Morocco in 1958, along with the return of Ifni in 1969.

Muhammad VI has been the ruler of Morocco since 1999.

History

Morocco's development has been shaped by various historical events. Berber peoples arrived between 4000 and 2000 BCE, followed by the Phoenicians, Romans, Vandals, and Arabs, who transformed the country into an Islamic society.

During the 19th century, Morocco integrated into the capitalist world economy but became subject to increasing foreign occupation and financial subservience to Europe. France secured its preponderance in Morocco between 1900 and 1904, and the country was officially divided into a protectorate under France and a protectorate under Spain in 1912.

Moroccan nationalism gained momentum after World War II, and the country gained independence in 1956. King Hassan's rule was characterized by political repression, including the marginalization of the Berber population, and a failed coup attempt in 1971. In the same year, Morocco embarked on a project to recover Western Sahara, which led to a crisis with Spain and a long-standing guerrilla war with the Sahrawis.

From 1992 onward, political reforms were introduced, including greater participation of opposition parties and the accession of Muhammad VI to the throne in 1999, who continued to further political reforms and free political prisoners.

Geography and Climate

Morocco is a country covering an area of 178,620 square miles (446,550 sq km) and is characterized by two major geographical features: the Atlas Mountains and the Sahara Desert. The Atlas Mountains run from southwest to northeast, dividing the country into different regions.

This mountain range comprises the High, Middle, and Saharan ranges, as well as the Rif Mountains that run along the Mediterranean coast of Morocco. The Gharb plains, located in the northern Atlantic coastal region, are the main agricultural areas. Other important plains include the Tadla plain along the Oum al-Rbi'a River south of Casablanca, the Haouz plain near Marrakech along the Tensift River, and the Sous River valley in the southwest. These rivers, which are only navigable by small boats, are used for irrigation purposes. The Mediterranean and Atlantic coasts experience mild, moist winters and hot, dry summers.

In contrast, the eastern and southern parts of Morocco have semi-arid climates that are largely influenced by the Sahara's heat and winds. The higher elevations of the Atlas Mountains, particularly the High Atlas region between Marrakech and Ouarzazate, are characterized by extremely cold temperatures, with snow covering the peaks throughout the year. Mount Toubkal, Morocco's highest peak, is located near Marrakech and is a popular destination for skiing enthusiasts.

People, Language, and Religion

Morocco has a population of around 30 million people, with over half living in urban areas. The population is relatively young, with nearly 48% under 21. Illiteracy rates are high, with 34.4% of men and 62.8% of women unable to read or write. The majority work in agriculture and fisheries, but there's a growing number in tourism, commerce, industry, and government.

The three primary ethnic groups are Arabs, mixed Arab-Berbers, and Berbers. Arabic is the official language, but French is also widely spoken. Sunni Islam is the state religion, and there is a small Jewish community.

Islamism appears to be on the rise, with the Party of Justice and Development being the third most powerful political party in the Chamber of Representatives. There have been reports of Islamist armed groups in Morocco with possible links to transnational Islamism, and a terrorist attack in Casablanca in 2003 was attributed to an Islamist group.

Economy

Morocco has been plagued by droughts since 1992, impacting the agricultural sector that employs 40% of the workforce and contributes over 15% to GDP. Manufacturing relies heavily on phosphate production but has suffered due to rising fuel costs and falling export earnings. Tourism is a significant source of foreign currency and employment.

Emigration is seen as a solution for unemployment, with millions of Moroccans living in Europe and sending remittances back home. Urban unemployment remains high, and foreign debt is nearly $18 billion.

Privatization of state-owned companies has been encouraged by the IMF and World Bank, but the government still maintains a costly food subsidy program.

Morocco's Top Tourist Destinations

Morocco is a vibrant and diverse country with a rich culture and many different experiences to offer.

The sound of the Call to Prayer can be heard throughout the day from Mosques, and the warm weather and varied landscapes create a stunning backdrop for exploration. From bustling markets and traditional crafts to stunning beaches and historical ruins, there is something for every traveler to enjoy.

While there may be many options to consider when planning a trip, the variety of experiences means that everyone can find something that suits their interests. Here are some of the top tourist destinations in Morocco:

1. Marrakech

Marrakech is a vibrant city located in the western part of Morocco, at the foothills of the Atlas Mountains. It is a popular tourist destination known for its beautiful architecture, colorful markets, and rich cultural heritage.

One of the most famous landmarks in Marrakech is the Jemaa el-fnaa Square, which is the main square in the city and a hub of activity day and night. The square is surrounded by bustling souks (markets) selling a wide variety of goods, including spices, textiles, ceramics, and jewelry. Visitors can also find traditional street performers, such as snake charmers, acrobats, and musicians, in the square.

Another popular attraction in Marrakech is the Koutoubia Mosque, which is the largest mosque in the city and one of the most beautiful examples of Islamic architecture in Morocco. Visitors can also explore the Bahia Palace, which is a stunning 19th-century palace with beautifully landscaped gardens and ornate rooms filled with intricate tile work and carvings.

Marrakech is also famous for its hammams, which are traditional Moroccan steam baths that offer a relaxing and rejuvenating experience. Visitors can enjoy a variety of treatments, including massages, exfoliations, and body wraps, in these traditional bathhouses.

Finally, visitors to Marrakech should also sample the local cuisine, which is a delicious blend of North African, Mediterranean, and Middle Eastern flavors. Some popular dishes to try include tagine (a slow-cooked stew), couscous (a dish made with steamed semolina), and pastilla (a sweet and savory pastry filled with meat and almonds).

Overall, Marrakech is a vibrant and exciting destination that offers visitors a unique blend of history, culture, and adventure.

2. Fes

Fes (also spelled Fez) is a city located in northern Morocco, and it is one of the country's most historic and culturally significant cities. It is known for its ancient medina (old town), which is a UNESCO World Heritage Site and home to many historical and architectural treasures.

The Medina of Fes is one of the largest car-free urban areas in the world, and it is a maze of narrow alleyways, bustling souks (markets), and beautiful mosques and madrasas (Islamic schools). The Al-Qarawiyyin Mosque and University, founded in the 9th century, is one of the oldest continually operating universities in the world and is located in the heart of Medina.

Other notable attractions in Fes include the Bou Inania Madrasa, the Dar Batha Museum, and the Royal Palace of Fes. The city is also known for its traditional crafts, such as ceramics, leatherwork, and textiles, which can be found in the souks.

Overall, Fes is a fascinating destination for travelers who are interested in history, architecture, and cultural experiences.

3. Casablanca

Casablanca is a city located in western Morocco, along the Atlantic Ocean. It is the largest city in Morocco and is the country's economic and cultural center. Casablanca has a rich history and is known for its unique blend of traditional Moroccan and modern European architecture.

Some of the most popular tourist attractions in Casablanca include the Hassan II Mosque, which is the largest mosque in Morocco and one of the largest in the world. The Casablanca Cathedral, which was built in 1930 and is one of the few examples of neo-gothic architecture in Morocco, is also a popular attraction.

Other notable sites in Casablanca include the Casablanca Twin Center, which is a pair of skyscrapers that dominate the city's skyline, and the Old Medina, which is the city's historic center and is home to a variety of shops and cafes.

Casablanca is also known for its vibrant nightlife, with many bars and nightclubs located throughout the city. Overall, it is a popular destination for tourists who want to experience the unique culture and history of Morocco while also enjoying modern amenities and attractions.

4. Sahara Desert

The Sahara Desert in Morocco is one of the largest hot deserts in the world, covering a vast area of around 9 million square kilometers across North Africa. Morocco is located in the northwest corner of the African continent, and its Sahara Desert region covers a significant part of the country's southeastern region.

The Moroccan Sahara Desert is known for its diverse landscape, ranging from vast dunes to rocky plateaus, valleys, and mountains. Some of the most notable landmarks in the Moroccan Sahara Desert include Erg Chebbi, a massive dune field that attracts tourists from all over the world, the Draa Valley, famous for its ancient kasbahs and date palm groves, and the Jebel Saghro, a mountain range that offers incredible trekking and hiking opportunities.

The Moroccan Sahara is also home to several nomadic communities, who have lived in the region for centuries, and their traditional way of life and cultural heritage is an integral part of the desert's identity. The region is also rich in history, with ancient trading routes, fortified cities, and archaeological sites that reflect the area's long and fascinating past.

5. Chefchaouen

Chefchaouen is a picturesque city located in the northwest of Morocco, near the Rif Mountains. It is known for its vibrant blue buildings and narrow streets that attract many tourists every year.

The city's blue-painted buildings are said to have been introduced by Jewish refugees in the 1930s, and today they give Chefchaouen a unique and charming character. The city is also known for its traditional markets, where visitors can find handmade crafts, textiles, and delicious local food.

Chefchaouen is also a popular destination for hikers and nature enthusiasts, as it is surrounded by beautiful mountains and valleys. There are many hiking trails and guided tours available, allowing visitors to explore the area's natural beauty.

Overall, Chefchaouen is a must-visit destination in Morocco for its stunning blue architecture, vibrant culture, and breathtaking natural scenery.

6. Essaouira

Essaouira is a coastal city located in the western part of Morocco, facing the Atlantic Ocean. The city has a rich history and cultural heritage, dating back to the 8th century, and it was recognized as a UNESCO World Heritage Site in 2001.

The city was formerly known as Mogador and has a long history of being a major port for trade between Morocco and Europe. Its strategic location made it a desirable location for many cultures and civilizations, including the Phoenicians, Carthaginians, Romans, and Portuguese.

Essaouira is known for its beautiful beaches, unique architecture, and cultural landmarks. Visitors can explore the city's medina, which is surrounded by fortified walls and includes many traditional markets, artisanal shops, and restaurants serving delicious Moroccan cuisine. The medina is also home to many historic landmarks, including the Moulay Hassan Square, the Skala de la Ville, and the Essaouira Citadel.

One of the most popular activities in Essaouira is surfing, as the city is known for its consistent waves and strong winds. Visitors can also enjoy kite surfing, windsurfing, and other water sports. Additionally, Essaouira is famous for its music and arts festivals, such as the Gnaoua World Music Festival and the Essaouira Alizes Festival.

Overall, Essaouira is a vibrant and culturally rich city that offers visitors a unique experience and a glimpse into Morocco's rich history and traditions.

7. Ouarzazate

Ouarzazate is a city in the south-central region of Morocco, known as the "door of the desert." It is a popular tourist destination due to its proximity to the Atlas Mountains and the Sahara Desert, as well as its stunning architecture and film studios.

The city has a rich history, dating back to the 11th century when it was a trading hub for caravans passing through the Sahara. Today, it is a thriving city with a population of around 100,000 people, and it is home to many cultural and historical landmarks, including the Taourirt Kasbah, a fortified palace that was once home to the Glaoui family.

One of the most notable attractions in Ouarzazate is the Atlas Film Studios, which is one of the largest movie studios in the world. The studio has been used to film many famous movies, including "Gladiator," "Lawrence of Arabia," and "Game of Thrones." Visitors can take a tour of the studio and see the various sets and props used in these films.

Other popular activities in Ouarzazate include exploring the nearby Ait Benhaddou, a UNESCO World Heritage Site that is known for its traditional architecture and stunning views of the surrounding landscape. Visitors can also go on a desert excursion, which may include camel riding, sandboarding, and stargazing.

Overall, Ouarzazate is a unique and beautiful city that offers visitors a glimpse into Morocco's rich culture and history, as well as its stunning natural landscapes.

8. Atlas Mountains

The Atlas Mountains are a mountain range that spans Morocco, Algeria, and Tunisia. In Morocco, the Atlas Mountains are a popular tourist destination due to their stunning scenery, rich culture, and diverse wildlife.

The Atlas Mountains are divided into three main ranges: the High Atlas, the Middle Atlas, and the Anti-Atlas. The High Atlas is the largest and tallest of the three, with several peaks over 4,000 meters, including Toubkal, the highest mountain in North Africa at 4,167 meters.

The Atlas Mountains are known for their rugged beauty and unique landscapes, which include snow-capped peaks, deep gorges, and lush valleys. The mountains are also home to many Berber villages and communities, where visitors can experience traditional Moroccan culture and hospitality.

One of the most popular activities in the Atlas Mountains is trekking, with many trails and routes available for all levels of experience. Visitors can trek through the mountains on their own or join a guided tour with a local guide, who can offer insights into the local culture and wildlife.

Other popular activities in the Atlas Mountains include rock climbing, mountain biking, and skiing during the winter months. The mountains are also home to several natural hot springs and spas, where visitors can relax and unwind after a day of outdoor activities.

Overall, the Atlas Mountains offer visitors a unique and breathtaking experience, with stunning scenery, rich culture, and diverse wildlife, making it a must-visit destination for any traveler to Morocco.

9. Rabat

Rabat is the capital city of Morocco, located on the Atlantic Ocean coast in the northwest of the country. The city has a rich history and cultural heritage, dating back to the 12th century when it was founded as a military fortress.

Today, Rabat is a vibrant city with a population of over one million people. The city is known for its stunning architecture, beautiful beaches, and rich cultural landmarks, including UNESCO World Heritage Sites such as the Kasbah of the Udayas and the Chellah Necropolis.

One of the most notable landmarks in Rabat is the Hassan Tower, a minaret of an incomplete mosque that was originally planned to be the largest in the world. The tower is now a symbol of the city and a popular tourist destination, offering stunning views of the surrounding landscape from its top.

Another popular attraction in Rabat is the Medina, which is an old town that dates back to the 17th century. The Medina is full of traditional markets, artisanal shops, and restaurants serving delicious Moroccan cuisine, making it a great place to experience the local culture and way of life.

Rabat is also known for its beaches, including the famous Bouregreg Beach, which offers visitors the chance to swim, surf, and relax on the golden sand. Additionally, Rabat is home to many museums and art galleries, such as the Museum Mohamed VI of Modern and Contemporary Art, which showcases the best of Moroccan and international art.

Overall, Rabat is a unique and beautiful city that offers visitors a diverse range of attractions and experiences, making it a must-visit destination for anyone traveling to Morocco.

10. Agadir

Agadir is a coastal city located in the southwestern region of Morocco, on the shores of the Atlantic Ocean. The city is known for its beautiful beaches, warm weather, and laid-back atmosphere, making it a popular tourist destination.

Agadir has a relatively short history compared to other Moroccan cities, as it was completely rebuilt after a devastating earthquake in 1960. As a result, the city has a modern and contemporary feel, with wide boulevards, modern architecture, and a range of international hotels and restaurants.

One of the main attractions in Agadir is its long sandy beach, which stretches for over 10 kilometers and is perfect for swimming, sunbathing, and water sports such as surfing and jet-skiing. The beach is also home to many beachfront cafes and restaurants, serving delicious local seafood and international cuisine.

Agadir is also known for its vibrant nightlife, with many bars, nightclubs, and music venues scattered throughout the city. Visitors can enjoy live music, dance the night away, or simply relax with a drink and soak up the atmosphere.

In addition to its beaches and nightlife, Agadir offers a range of other attractions and activities, including the Agadir Oufella Ruins, which offer stunning panoramic views of the city and surrounding landscape, and the Souk El Had, a traditional market selling everything from spices and textiles to leather goods and handicrafts.

Overall, Agadir is a beautiful and lively city that offers visitors a unique and memorable

Moroccan experience, with a mix of modern and traditional culture, beautiful beaches, and a vibrant atmosphere.

11. Ait Ben Haddou

Ait Ben Haddou is a fortified village located in the southeastern part of Morocco, near the city of Ouarzazate. The village is famous for its stunning architecture and unique earthen buildings, which have been featured in many films and TV shows, including Game of Thrones.

Ait Ben Haddou is a UNESCO World Heritage Site and is considered one of the best-preserved examples of earthen architecture in the world. The village is made up of several kasbahs, or fortified houses, which were built using a technique of rammed earth and straw that has been used in the region for centuries.

The kasbahs are connected by narrow alleys and stairways, and the whole village is surrounded by high walls for protection. The largest and most impressive kasbah in Ait Ben Haddou is the Kasbah of Ait Ben Haddou, which is now partly in ruins but is still a popular tourist attraction.

Visitors to Ait Ben Haddou can take a guided tour of the village, explore its narrow streets, visit the kasbahs, and learn about the traditional way of life in the region. The village is also surrounded by stunning natural scenery, including the Atlas Mountains and the Draa Valley, making it a popular destination for hiking and outdoor activities.

Overall, Ait Ben Haddou is a unique and beautiful village that offers visitors a glimpse into the rich history and culture of Morocco, with its stunning earthen architecture and beautiful natural surroundings. It's a must-visit destination for anyone traveling to the region.

12. Dades Valley

The Dades Valley, also known as the Valley of the Dades, is a picturesque valley located in the High Atlas Mountains of Morocco. The valley is famous for its stunning natural beauty, with its red and orange rock formations, lush greenery, and rushing rivers.

The Dades Valley is popular among hikers and outdoor enthusiasts, as it offers a range of hiking trails and outdoor activities, including trekking, mountain biking, and rock climbing. The valley is also home to several Berber villages, where visitors can learn about the traditional way of life in the region and sample local cuisine.

One of the most popular attractions in the Dades Valley is the Dades Gorge, a deep canyon that stretches for over 25 kilometers and offers breathtaking views of the surrounding landscape. Visitors can hike along the canyon, taking in the stunning rock formations and waterfalls, or simply relax and soak up the natural beauty.

Another popular attraction in the Dades Valley is the Valley of Roses, a region located to the north of the valley that is famous for its rose gardens and production of rosewater and other rose-based products. Visitors can explore the gardens, learn about the rose harvesting and production process, and purchase locally-made rose products to take home as souvenirs.

Overall, the Dades Valley is a beautiful and unique destination that offers visitors a range of outdoor activities and cultural experiences, making it a must-visit destination for anyone traveling to Morocco.

13. Tangier

Tangier is a port city located in the northernmost part of Morocco, overlooking the Strait of Gibraltar and the Mediterranean Sea. The city has a rich history, with influences from the Phoenicians, Romans, and Arabs, and is known for its vibrant culture and unique blend of European and African influences.

One of the main attractions in Tangier is its medina, a walled old city that is home to a maze of narrow streets, colorful markets, and traditional architecture. Visitors can explore the medina's winding alleys, visit its mosques and palaces, and sample the local cuisine at its many street-side cafes and restaurants.

Tangier is also known for its stunning beaches, with long stretches of white sand and crystal-clear waters. The city's beaches offer a range of activities, including swimming, sunbathing, and water sports such as windsurfing and kiteboarding.

Another popular attraction in Tangier is the Kasbah Museum, a former palace that now houses a collection of artifacts and exhibits related to Moroccan history and culture. Visitors can learn about the country's rich heritage, including its traditional crafts, architecture, and art.

Tangier is also a gateway to other popular destinations in Morocco, such as Chefchaouen, a beautiful blue-painted town nestled in the Rif Mountains, and the ancient Roman ruins of Volubilis.

Overall, Tangier is a vibrant and fascinating city that offers visitors a unique and memorable Moroccan experience, with its blend of European and African influences, stunning beaches, and rich history and culture.

14. Meknes

Meknes is a city located in northern Morocco, about 130 km east of Rabat. It is known for its rich history and stunning architecture and is a popular tourist destination in Morocco.

One of the main attractions in Meknes is the old Medina, a walled city that dates back to the 17th century and is a UNESCO World Heritage Site. Visitors can explore the medina's narrow streets, visit its markets and souks, and see its stunning architecture, including the Bab el-Mansour gate, which is considered one of the most beautiful gates in the country.

Another popular attraction in Meknes is the Mausoleum of Moulay Ismail, a grand tomb that houses the remains of the Moroccan king Moulay Ismail. The mausoleum is known for its stunning architecture, with intricate tile work and carvings, and is considered one of the most important religious sites in Morocco.

Meknes is also home to several beautiful palaces and gardens, including the Dar Jamai Museum, which is housed in a stunning 19th-century palace and showcases Moroccan art and culture, and the Agdal Gardens, a vast green space that features fountains, orchards, and stunning views of the city.

Visitors to Meknes can also take a day trip to nearby Volubilis, a well-preserved Roman city that dates back to the 3rd century BC. The city is home to stunning ruins, including the remains of temples, baths, and houses, and is a popular destination for history and archaeology enthusiasts.

Overall, Meknes is a beautiful and historic city that offers visitors a range of cultural and historical experiences, making it a must-visit destination for anyone traveling to Morocco.

15. Volubilis

Volubilis is an ancient Roman city located in northern Morocco, about 30 km north of the city of Meknes. The city dates back to the 3rd century BC and was an important center of trade and agriculture in Roman Africa.

Today, Volubilis is a UNESCO World Heritage Site and a popular tourist destination in Morocco. Visitors to the site can explore the ruins of the ancient city, which include well-preserved buildings and structures such as temples, forums, basilicas, and triumphal arches.

One of the most impressive structures in Volubilis is the Arch of Caracalla, a triumphal arch that was built in the early 3rd century AD to commemorate the Roman Emperor Caracalla's victories over the local Berber tribes. The arch is decorated with intricate carvings and reliefs, depicting scenes of Roman military conquests and local life.

Another notable feature of Volubilis is its well-preserved mosaic floors, which feature intricate designs and patterns that offer a glimpse into the daily life and culture of the ancient city's inhabitants. The mosaics can be found in the ruins of private residences and public buildings throughout the site.

Visitors to Volubilis can also learn about the city's history and culture at the on-site museum, which features a collection of artifacts and exhibits related to the site's Roman and Berber heritage.

Overall, Volubilis is a fascinating and unique destination that offers visitors a glimpse into Morocco's rich history and cultural heritage, making it a must-visit destination for anyone traveling to the region.

16. Merzouga

Merzouga is a small town located in southeastern Morocco, on the edge of the Sahara Desert. It is known for its stunning desert landscapes, including towering dunes and vast expanses of golden sand.

One of the main attractions in Merzouga is the Erg Chebbi dunes, a series of towering dunes that reach heights of up to 150 meters. Visitors to Merzouga can take a camel trek into the desert to explore the dunes and experience the unique beauty of the Sahara.

Another popular activity in Merzouga is stargazing. The town is located in a remote area with very little light pollution, making it an ideal location for observing the night sky. Visitors can take a guided tour of the desert at night and marvel at the stars and constellations visible in the clear desert sky.

Merzouga is also home to several traditional Berber villages, where visitors can learn about the local culture and way of life. Many of the villages offer homestay accommodations, allowing visitors to experience traditional Berber hospitality and cuisine.

Visitors to Merzouga can also take a day trip to nearby destinations, such as the Todra Gorge, a stunning canyon with towering red cliffs and a river running through it, or the Dades Valley, a beautiful valley known for its winding roads and stunning rock formations.

Overall, Merzouga is a unique and unforgettable destination that offers visitors a chance to experience the beauty and culture of the Sahara Desert, making it a must-visit destination for anyone traveling to Morocco.

17. El Jadida

El Jadida is a coastal city located in western Morocco, about 100 km southwest of Casablanca. It is known for its beautiful beaches, historic architecture, and cultural heritage.

One of the main attractions in El Jadida is the Portuguese Cistern, a historic underground water reservoir that was built in the 16th century during the Portuguese occupation of the city. The cistern features a unique architectural style, with vaulted ceilings and columns that support the roof. Visitors can explore the cistern and learn about its history and significance to the city.

Another popular attraction in El Jadida is the Mazagan Fortress, a historic fortress that was built in the 16th century to protect the city from invasion. The fortress features a mix of

Portuguese and Moroccan architectural styles and is a UNESCO World Heritage Site. Visitors can explore the fortress and learn about its history and role in the city's development.

El Jadida is also known for its beautiful beaches, which offer a range of activities such as swimming, sunbathing, and water sports. Some of the most popular beaches in the area include Sidi Bouzid Beach and El Haouzia Beach.

Visitors to El Jadida can also experience the city's vibrant culture and cuisine by exploring its markets and trying traditional Moroccan dishes such as tagine and couscous. The city is known for its fresh seafood, and visitors can sample a range of local seafood dishes at the city's restaurants and cafes.

Overall, El Jadida is a beautiful and historic city that offers visitors a range of cultural and recreational activities, making it a must-visit destination for anyone traveling to Morocco.

18. Ifrane

Ifrane is a small town located in the Middle Atlas Mountains of Morocco, about 65 km south of Fez. It is known for its beautiful alpine landscapes, architecture, and cultural heritage.

One of the main attractions in Ifrane is its natural beauty. The town is surrounded by cedar forests, mountain ranges, and rolling hills, making it an ideal destination for hiking, skiing, and other outdoor activities. Visitors can explore the nearby Ifrane National Park, which is home to a variety of wildlife, including Barbary macaques, wild boars, and Atlas deer.

Ifrane is also known for its unique architecture, which features a mix of traditional Moroccan and European styles. The town was built in the 1930s by the

French colonial authorities as a retreat from the heat of the Moroccan plains. Visitors can explore the town's charming streets and squares, which are lined with distinctive red-roofed buildings and ornate fountains.

Another popular attraction in Ifrane is Al Akhawayn University, a prestigious university that was founded in 1993. The university features a beautiful campus with modern facilities and is known for its strong academic programs and diverse student body.

Visitors to Ifrane can also experience the town's vibrant culture by visiting its markets and trying traditional Moroccan dishes such as tagine, couscous, and mint tea. Ifrane is also known for its handicrafts, including pottery, rugs, and wood carvings.

Overall, Ifrane is a beautiful and unique destination that offers visitors a chance to experience the natural beauty, culture, and heritage of Morocco, making it a must-visit destination for anyone traveling to the region.

19. Toubkal National Park

Toubkal National Park is a protected area located in the High Atlas Mountains of Morocco, about 70 km south of Marrakech. The park covers an area of over 380 square kilometers and is home to the highest peak in North Africa, Mount Toubkal, which stands at 4,167 meters above sea level.

The park is known for its stunning alpine landscapes, including mountain peaks, valleys, and gorges. Visitors can explore the park's hiking trails, which offer spectacular views of the surrounding mountains and valleys. The most popular hike is the ascent of Mount Toubkal, which can be done as a day trip or as part of a multi-day trek.

The park is also home to a variety of flora and fauna, including the Atlas cedar, juniper trees, and several species of birds and mammals. Visitors can spot Barbary macaques, foxes, and even the occasional wild boar.

One of the main attractions in the park is the Berber villages, which are scattered throughout the mountainous terrain. These villages offer visitors a chance to experience traditional Berber culture and hospitality, as well as to try local dishes such as tagine and couscous.

Overall, Toubkal National Park is a beautiful and unique destination that offers visitors a chance to experience the natural beauty, culture, and heritage of Morocco. The park is a must-visit destination for anyone interested in hiking, outdoor activities, or simply enjoying the stunning alpine scenery of North Africa.

20. Skoura Oasis

Skoura Oasis is a beautiful and historic oasis located in the Draa Valley of Morocco. It is situated between the High Atlas Mountains and the Sahara Desert and is known for its lush palm groves, stunning kasbahs (fortified houses), and rich history.

The oasis is home to over 700,000 palm trees and is one of the largest oases in Morocco. It has been an important agricultural center for centuries, with crops including dates, almonds, figs, and pomegranates. The oasis also has several traditional Moroccan gardens, known as "Jardins," which are designed to provide shade and relaxation for visitors.

One of the highlights of Skoura Oasis is the Kasbah Amridil, a beautifully preserved kasbah that dates back to the 17th century.

The Kasbah is open to visitors and offers a fascinating glimpse into traditional Moroccan architecture and design. Other notable kasbahs in the oasis include Kasbah Ait Ben Moro and Kasbah Ben Abbou.

In addition to exploring the kasbahs and gardens, visitors to Skoura Oasis can also go on guided camel treks, hike in the nearby mountains, or take a 4x4 tour of the desert. The oasis is also a popular spot for birdwatching, with several bird species that are unique to the region.

Overall, Skoura Oasis is a beautiful and fascinating destination that offers a unique glimpse into Moroccan history and culture.

Where to Stay in Morocco

Morocco has a wide range of accommodation options to suit different budgets and preferences. Here are some popular places to stay in Morocco:

1. Marrakech:

This vibrant city has a mix of traditional Moroccan riads, luxury hotels, and budget-friendly hostels. The old town, or Medina, is a popular place to stay to experience the local culture and atmosphere.

2. Fes:

Known for its historic medina and traditional architecture, Fes has a range of accommodation options, including charming riads and hotels.

3. Chefchaouen:

This picturesque blue-painted town is a popular destination for travelers seeking a peaceful retreat. There are many cozy guesthouses and boutique hotels to choose from.

4. Essaouira:

This coastal town is known for its relaxed atmosphere and stunning beaches. There are many guesthouses and hotels available, ranging from budget-friendly to luxury options.

5. Casablanca:

Morocco's largest city has a mix of modern hotels and traditional riads. It's a good base for exploring the city and nearby attractions.

6. Sahara Desert:

For a unique experience, consider staying in a desert camp to experience the magic of the Sahara. These camps offer a range of accommodations, from traditional Bedouin tents to luxury glamping options.

Overall, Morocco has a variety of accommodation options to suit different preferences and budgets, so it's worth researching and comparing options to find the best fit for your needs.

Morocco Travel Expenses

Accommodation – In big cities such as Marrakesh and Fez, dorm rooms with 6-8 beds are available for 80-110 MAD per night. In smaller areas, the cost for such rooms is around 50-60 MAD. Private rooms at hostels are also available at a price range of 260-380 MAD per night, with free Wi-Fi and breakfast often included.

For budget hotels in Marrakesh and Fez, expect to pay around 270-410 MAD per night for a double room, which comes with basic amenities such as free Wi-Fi, TV, free breakfast, and sometimes an outdoor pool.

Wild camping is allowed in Morocco for those who bring a tent. However, locals may not appreciate it if you camp too close to their property, so be mindful of your surroundings. It is not uncommon for nomads or police officers to check on you during your stay.

Food – Moroccan cuisine is a blend of various culinary traditions, including Berber, Andalusian, Mediterranean, French, and sub-Saharan. Spices are widely used, with the traditional ras el hanout mix consisting of 27 different spices. Common meats include beef, goat, and lamb, usually served with couscous, while fish like mackerel and anchovy are popular in coastal areas. Pastilla is a must-try pastry filled with meat or seafood.

Eating in Morocco can be very affordable, particularly if you opt for market food. A pot of mint tea costs 8-10 MAD, while local dishes like tagine range from 35-55 MAD. Seafood dishes in coastal cities like Essaouira are more expensive, with a fish dish costing about 100-150 MAD and a lobster around 350-400 MAD. Western-style or touristy restaurants tend to be pricier, with main dishes starting at around 150 MAD. Beer and wine cost around 70 MAD per drink.

Grocery shopping in Morocco is not necessary as food is cheap and eating out is convenient. However, if you choose to buy groceries, expect to pay around 200 MAD per week for basic items such as pasta, vegetables, and chicken.

Transportation - Taxis start at 7 MAD in cities, buses cost around 5 MAD for local rides and up to 100 MAD for intercity travel, train fares vary by distance and class with second-class tickets from Casablanca to Marrakech around 80-100 MAD, and rental cars start at 250 MAD per day. Prices are subject to change, and bargaining is common.

Backpacking Morocco recommended expenses

For backpackers, a budget of 285 MAD per day is recommended. This includes staying in hostels, eating at market stalls and cooking some meals, limiting alcohol consumption, using local transportation, and doing free and low-cost activities.

For mid-range budget travelers, a budget of 525 MAD per day is suggested. This includes staying in private Airbnb accommodations, eating out for all meals, taking trains for transportation, and participating in more paid activities like museum visits and camping in the Sahara.

For those on a luxury budget of 1,120 MAD or more per day, they can stay in hotels, eat out at any restaurant, enjoy drinks, travel between cities by flying or hiring a driver, and choose from a range of tours and activities. However, this is only the starting point for luxury travel.

Morocco Tourist Tips

Here are some practical tips for tourists traveling to Morocco:

1. Dress conservatively:

Morocco is a predominantly Muslim country, so it's important to dress conservatively, especially if you're a woman. Avoid revealing clothing and opt for long sleeves and pants.

2. Learn some basic Arabic or French:

While many Moroccans speak English, it's always helpful to learn some basic Arabic or French phrases to help with communication. It's also a great way to show respect for the local culture.

3. Be prepared for the weather:

Morocco can be hot in the summer, so pack light clothing and sunscreen. In the winter, it can get cold, especially in the mountains, so bring warm layers.

4. Bargain when shopping:

Bargaining is a common practice in Morocco, especially in markets and souks. Don't be afraid to negotiate prices, but be respectful and keep in mind that many vendors rely on the income from their sales.

5. Watch out for scams:

Like in any tourist destination, there are scams to watch out for in Morocco. Be wary of people offering unsolicited help or trying to sell you something you didn't ask for. Stick to reputable tour companies and be cautious when using taxis or public transportation.

6. **Respect local customs and traditions**:

Moroccans are proud of their culture and traditions, so it's important to respect them. For example, always remove your shoes before entering a mosque or someone's home, and avoid public displays of affection.

7. **Try the local cuisine:**

Moroccan cuisine is delicious and varied, so be sure to try local dishes like tagine, couscous, and pastilla. You'll find plenty of street food vendors and restaurants to choose from.

8. **Stay hydrated:**

It's important to stay hydrated, especially if you're traveling during the summer months. Drink bottled water and carry a reusable water bottle to refill when needed.

9. Bring cash:

While many places accept credit cards, it's always a good idea to have cash on hand. ATMs can be found in most cities and towns, but it's a good idea to notify your bank before traveling to avoid any issues with your account.

10.   Be mindful of your safety:

Morocco is generally a safe country to travel to, but it's always important to be mindful of your surroundings. Keep an eye on your belongings, especially in crowded areas, and avoid walking alone at night.

Morocco's Money Saving Tips

Traveling in Morocco doesn't necessarily require a lot of money, although there are opportunities to spend more if you wish. To save money while traveling in Morocco, here are some tips:

1. Eat from street stalls:

Finding affordable meals in Morocco is effortless, with restaurant meals available for as low as 30 MAD. However, the cheapest option is street food, which includes mouth-watering kebabs, sausages, roasted chicken, barbecued corn, and large sandwiches that cost only a few dollars. To save money on food, it's best to eat at the local markets in Medina.

2. Negotiate your cab fare:

Before getting into a taxi in Morocco, make sure to negotiate the fare as there are no set prices, and bargaining is necessary. To avoid getting overcharged, it's advisable to ask for price estimates from hotel or hostel staff.

3. Avoid false guides:

In the medinas of Morocco, there are fake guides who offer tour services. If approached by them, firmly decline and walk away as they can be persistent. However, if you continue to walk away, they eventually give up.

4. Be careful of thieves:

Petty theft is a common problem in Morocco's crowded medinas, with wallets, watches, and cameras being the most commonly stolen items. It's important to remain vigilant and keep your valuables hidden to avoid becoming a victim of theft.

5. Avoid drinking:

Despite the disapproval of drinking in Morocco, there are still establishments that serve alcohol, albeit at a premium price and with limited drink options. It's recommended to refrain from drinking during your visit to Morocco, both to save money and to respect the local culture.

6. Stay with a local:

Couchsurfing is a great option to save money and gain a better understanding of the local culture. By staying with a local, you can get insider tips and a deeper insight into the city, making it a worthwhile experience.

7. Bring a water bottle:

Although tap water in Morocco is generally considered safe for drinking, it's recommended to bring a reusable water bottle with a built-in filter as a precaution. LifeStraw is a reliable brand that provides water bottles with built-in filters, ensuring that your drinking water is always clean and safe.

8. Plan:

To reduce expenses on travel, it is advisable to plan by researching different options, comparing prices, and making early reservations for flights, accommodations, and activities. This approach can help you secure the most favorable deals.

9. Avoid tourist traps:

To avoid overpriced tourist traps, it's essential to conduct some research and discover authentic experiences that are budget-friendly. Seek recommendations from locals and venture out to less popular destinations.

How to Travel Around Morocco

Public transportation – Public transportation in Morocco may not be reliable in some areas. While bigger cities such as Marrakesh and Casablanca offer bus services, they are often old, overcrowded, and difficult to navigate. As an alternative, most locals prefer using petit taxis which are small vehicles that can accommodate up to three people and are widely available throughout the country.

The fares for petit taxis are inexpensive, although there may be an additional fee after 8 pm. It's best to negotiate the fare upfront to avoid any misunderstandings. Metered taxis are also available in larger cities like Marrakesh, with fares starting at around 7 MAD and an additional charge of 4 MAD per kilometer.

Grand taxis – Grand taxis in Morocco are shared vehicles that can accommodate up to six passengers and are commonly used for longer trips between neighboring towns or cities. These taxis wait until they are full before departing, but the wait times are usually not too long. They can be found near taxi stands, buses, or train stations. If you have a lot of luggage, you may need to pay an additional fee, and it's best to arrange the fare beforehand.

Bus – Intercity buses are an affordable and effective mode of transportation in Morocco, especially when compared to other options. The four primary bus operators are Supratours, CTM, SATAS (regional), and Ghazala (regional).

Of these, CTM and Supratours are the most dependable, offering comfortable buses with air conditioning. You can either buy your tickets online or directly at the bus station. However, the websites of these operators are not always efficient or reliable.

For instance, a 4-hour bus journey from Marrakesh to Casablanca usually costs around 75-110 MAD, whereas a 6.5-hour trip from Marrakesh to Tangier is usually priced at 260-275 MAD. The fare for a trip from Casablanca to Fez is around 95-120 MAD.

Train – ONCF operates Morocco's national rail network, connecting major cities such as Marrakesh, Casablanca, Rabat, Meknes, and Fez. The trains are comfortable and mostly punctual, although occasional disruptions may occur. A high-speed rail now runs between Casablanca and Fez. Schedules and fares can be accessed through ONCF.

The train ride from Marrakesh to Casablanca takes about 2.5 hours and costs approximately 50 MAD, while the journey from Marrakesh to Rabat, which takes 4.5 hours, starts around 150-180 MAD. Traveling from Casablanca to Fez takes 4 hours and is priced between 50-120 MAD. The trip from Fez to Marrakesh lasts 6.5 hours and costs 195 MAD.

Flying – The primary domestic airline in Morocco is Royal Air Maroc, which occasionally offers excellent discounts. A one-hour flight from Marrakesh to Casablanca usually starts at approximately 870 MAD, while a one-hour flight from Marrakesh to Fez costs around 520 MAD.

Car rental – Renting a car is not commonly suggested in Morocco due to aggressive driving and high accident rates. However, if you plan to explore lesser-known destinations, renting a car could be a viable option. Rental rates usually begin from 200 MAD per day or even less.

Group tour – For those who prefer to explore Morocco with a tour, The Nomadic Network is a recommended option. It is a tour company that specializes in offering affordable small-group tours to unique destinations for travelers who seek to experience a place beyond its touristy spots. The tours bring together adventurers from different parts of the world.

When to visit Morocco

Morocco's shoulder seasons are from April to May and September to November, which are the best times to visit the country. The weather is warm and pleasant, and there are fewer tourists. However, if you're planning to surf the coast or hike the Atlas Mountains, the best time to go is different.

Summer (June-August) can be unbearably hot, with temperatures above 35°C (95°F) in places like Marrakesh and Fez. During this time, many people prefer to visit the coast to escape the heat.

In winter (December-February), temperatures are mild but can drop to as low as -3°C (27°F) in Marrakesh and the Atlas Mountains receive heavy snowfall. Along the coast and in the north, winters are wet and not the best time to visit. The best time to hike in the

Atlas Mountains is during spring (April to May) and fall (September to October) when the weather is mild and there is little risk of severe weather. Summer is the best time to enjoy the coast, with temperatures up to 27°C (80°F) and the ocean breeze providing relief.

How to Stay Safe in Morocco

Morocco is generally a safe destination, but it's important to stay vigilant to avoid petty crime and harassment.

Women traveling alone should be especially cautious as they may attract unwanted attention.

Walking alone at night is not recommended in cities, and always arrange the price of a taxi in advance to avoid being ripped off. It's also important to be aware of common travel scams.

In case of emergency, dial 19 or 112 for mobile phones. Purchase good travel insurance as it provides comprehensive protection in case anything goes wrong.

To stay safe, keep an eye on your surroundings, avoid carrying valuables, be cautious of strangers offering help, and be aware of pickpockets.

Women should dress modestly and avoid walking alone at night. It's also recommended to go with reputable tour companies or knowledgeable guides when traveling to remote areas or going on a trek.

Adventurous Activities in Morocco

Morocco is a great destination for adventure seekers, with its diverse terrain, vibrant culture, and friendly people. Here are some adventurous activities to consider while in Morocco:

1. Hiking in the Atlas Mountains:

The Atlas Mountains offer some of the best hiking in Morocco, with stunning scenery and diverse terrain. You can hike independently or with a guide, and there are plenty of trails to suit all levels of fitness and experience.

2. Sandboarding in the Sahara:

The Sahara is the largest hot desert in the world and offers a unique sandboarding experience. You can ride down the dunes on a sandboard, similar to snowboarding but on the sand, and experience the thrill of the desert.

3. Hot air balloon ride over Marrakech:

Take a hot air balloon ride over the stunning city of Marrakech, and see the city from a unique perspective. This is a great way to experience the city's architecture and history, as well as the surrounding landscapes.

4. Surfing in Taghazout:

Taghazout is a small fishing village located on the coast of Morocco and is known for its excellent surfing conditions. There are plenty of surf schools and rental shops in the area, and you can also explore the local culture and cuisine.

5. Camel trekking in the Sahara:

Experience the desert like a local and ride a camel through the Sahara. You can take a guided trek through the desert, and camp overnight under the stars for a truly unforgettable experience.

6. Rock climbing in Todra Gorge:

Todra Gorge is a popular rock climbing destination, with a range of routes suitable for all levels of climbers. The area also offers stunning views and plenty of opportunities for hiking and exploring.

7. Quad biking in the desert:

Explore the desert on a quad bike and experience the thrill of off-road adventure. There are plenty of guided tours available, and you can also combine quad biking with other desert activities such as sandboarding and camel trekking.

8. Paragliding in the Atlas Mountains:

Take to the skies and paraglide over the stunning Atlas Mountains. This is a great way to experience the beauty of the mountains and get a unique perspective on the landscape.

There are many other adventurous activities to do in Morocco, depending on your interests and preferences. Be sure to research and plan, and always take necessary safety precautions.

MOROCCAN TOURIST VISA

On this page, you will discover information regarding the method of applying for a Morocco Tourist visa, such as the countries that need the visa, the essential criteria, and the expenses involved. Additionally, it will also address some regularly asked topics relating to Morocco visas.

1.1 Do You Need a Visa for Morocco?

It depends on your nationality if you need a visa to enter Morocco. Individuals from certain nations do not need to seek a visa in advance and may travel to Morocco without one. This exception applies to citizens of nations such as the United States, European Union member states, Japan, Australia, and others.

1.2 Visa-exempted nations

Whether or not a visa is necessary to go to Morocco for a stay of up to 90 days depends on one's nationality. Citizens of various countries, such as those in the European Union, the United States, Canada, Australia, Japan, and others, do not require a visa to visit Morocco.

Hong Kong and Singapore nationals may remain for a maximum of 30 days. Diplomatic, diplomatic, or service passport holders from various countries may travel to Morocco for up to 90 days without a visa.

Citizens of just three countries, the Republic of the Congo, Guinea, and Mali, are qualified for the Morocco Electronic Travel Authorization and may apply for it from anywhere in the globe. After acceptance, they must print it off and show it at the point of entrance and exit from Morocco.

1.3 How to Travel to Morocco if I Don't Need a Visa?

If you are a citizen of one of the mentioned countries, you don't need to apply for a visa to enter Morocco. You simply need to carry your passport, which must have at least one empty page for the entrance stamp and be valid for six more months, and a return-flight ticket within the following 90 days. If you desire to continue your stay, you may seek an extension at the local police station in Morocco.

1.4 What Type of Morocco Visa Should I Apply For?

The Morocco Tourist Visa, also known as a short-term visa, is provided to those who need a visa to enter Morocco and desire to visit for different objectives, including tourism, business, personal visits, cultural or academic activities, sporting events, journalism, or medical treatment, among others. The visa may be given for single or multiple entries and permits the traveler to remain for up to 90 days. Some nations are excluded from acquiring a tourist visa for Morocco.

2. Morocco Tourist visa

2.1 Required Documents for Morocco Visa

1. Passport

- Must have validity that transcends the date of the applicant's length of stay in Morocco.

- Identity card or residence permit, or document that shows the applicant's address.

- Photocopy of the passport information page.

2. Two photos

- Colored, shot against a white backdrop, size 4cm by 3cm, and showcasing the applicant's facial characteristics clearly

3. Bank statement, or recommendation letter from the Ministry of Tourism or a representative of the Moroccan National Tourist Office or request from an authorized travel agency, or in case of a family visit, a duly legalized attestation of invitation that guarantees any possible medical or repatriation expenses

4. Return ticket with a confirmed reservation

5. Travel Insurance

6. Hotel booking

7. Visa fee receipt

8. Completed visa application form

2.2 Morocco Visa Application Steps

1. **Gather the needed paperwork.**

2. **Fill out the Moroccan visa application form.**

   To complete the Moroccan visa application form, it is important to use capital letters and Latin characters.

Although the application form may be filled in Arabic, the applicant's first and last name as well as a place of birth must be written in Latin letters.

3. Schedule your Moroccan visa appointment.

To establish whether an appointment is required and how to arrange one, persons can call the Moroccan embassy or consulate.

4. Submit your printed Moroccan visa application form.

The completed visa application form, together with the relevant supporting papers and visa criteria, should be delivered in person to the Moroccan consulate, embassy, or visa application facility.

5. Pay the visa application cost.

2.3 Morocco Visa Fees

To get an ordinary Moroccan visa, you must pay a charge of DH220, which cannot be reimbursed even if your visa application is refused. Please be advised that extra costs may also be applied.

3.1 Where to Apply

Individuals seeking a Moroccan visa may apply via Moroccan consulates, embassies, or visa application facilities in their respective countries of citizenship or domicile. If there are no Moroccan representatives accessible in their nation, they may submit their visa application to the authorized diplomatic mission or Honorary Consul.

In case no such representative exists, applicants may contact the Moroccan Ministry of Foreign Affairs and International Cooperation directly, especially the Directorate of Consular and Social Affairs in Rabat, to get a visa at the airport.

3.2 Morocco Visa Processing Time

Normally, Moroccan visas are issued within 10 working days. However, in exceptional circumstances when extra data is necessary or in-depth examinations are needed, the procedure may take up to 30 days.

3.3 For approved visa applications

When applying for a visa, it is important to produce travel insurance, a confirmed return ticket, documentation of accommodation bookings or a voucher, and to pay the chancery costs. After getting the visa, it is necessary to check that the information on the visa matches that on the passport.

10 Days in Morocco

Morocco is a country that offers a diverse range of experiences to its visitors, including adventure, mystery, and natural beauty.

From walking with camels in the Sahara at sunrise to snowboarding in the Atlas Mountains in the afternoon, and relaxing in luxurious medina riads in the evening, Morocco has something for everyone.

Although the country is vast and travel distances can be long, the stunning destinations make it worthwhile. While many travelers aim to see all the highlights of Morocco in a week, taking a few extra days to explore at a more leisurely pace can provide a more fulfilling experience.

Some travelers choose to focus their time around an imperial city like Marrakesh, which serves as a gateway to the mountains and desert, while others seek off-the-beaten-track destinations like M'Goun Mountain, Demnate, Ouzoud waterfalls, Agdz oasis-town, and Tifnit beach.

By following a 10-day Morocco travel guide, visitors can make the most of their time and see the best that this fascinating country has to offer.

Day 1: Arrival in Casablanca

Upon arrival at Casablanca's Mohammed V International Airport, you can either take a taxi or a train to your hotel. Check in at your hotel and freshen up.

For breakfast or brunch, head to Cafe Bistro du Louvre and try some traditional Moroccan pastries and coffee if you didn't get to eat anything or had little to eat before starting your trip.

In the afternoon, visit the Hassan II Mosque, one of the largest mosques in the world. Guided tours are available, and it's a great way to learn about Moroccan culture and religion.

After visiting the mosque, take a stroll along the Corniche, a promenade that offers stunning views of the Atlantic Ocean.

For Lunch, head to Le Rouget de l'Isle, a seafood restaurant that offers traditional Moroccan dishes as well as French cuisine. You should rest for a while after eating.

In the evening, take a taxi to the city center and visit the Old Medina. The Medina is a UNESCO World Heritage site and offers a glimpse into the city's history and culture. Walk through the narrow alleys, and visit the traditional markets (souks) and shops selling handicrafts, spices, and textiles.

For dinner, try some traditional Moroccan cuisine at La Scala, a restaurant located in a beautiful garden setting with a relaxed atmosphere.

After dinner, you can either head back to your hotel or experience the vibrant nightlife of Casablanca. The city has several bars and nightclubs that offer live music and entertainment.

Where to stay:

For your stay in Casablanca, I recommend Hotel Kenzi Basma, a four-star hotel located in the city center that offers comfortable rooms and amenities.

Day 2: Rabat

On the second day of your trip go to Rabat, the capital city of Morocco. Start your day by having a hearty breakfast, try a Moroccan breakfast favorite, "baghrir" or Moroccan pancakes with butter and honey.

After breakfast, take an early morning train from Casablanca to Rabat (approx. 1-hour journey) and check in at your pre-booked hotel and freshen up or start exploring the city's beauty.

Upon arrival at Rabat, visit the Hassan Tower, a minaret of an incomplete mosque and an iconic landmark of Rabat.

Next, visit the Mausoleum of Mohammed V, the resting place of the former King of Morocco and his two sons.

Afterward, visit the Kasbah of the Udayas, an ancient fortress, and UNESCO World Heritage Site located at the mouth of the Bouregreg River.

For lunch, head to Dar Naji, a restaurant located inside the Kasbah, and try some traditional Moroccan tagine.

After lunch, visit the Chellah Necropolis, an ancient Roman and Islamic site that includes a complex of ruins, gardens, and storks.

Take a stroll along the picturesque Bouregreg Marina and enjoy the views of the river and boats.

For dinner, head to La Bodega, a Spanish-Moroccan restaurant located in the Hassan district that offers a unique blend of Spanish and Moroccan cuisine.

After dinner, you can explore the lively nightlife of Rabat. Head to the Agdal district, where you'll find plenty of bars, cafes, and nightclubs.

Where to stay:

For your stay in Rabat, I recommend the Hotel La Tour Hassan Palace, a luxurious five-star hotel located in the heart of the city that offers comfortable rooms and excellent amenities.

If you're looking for a budget-friendly option for your stay in Rabat, I will recommend the Auberge de Jeunesse de la Jeunesse de Rabat. This hostel is located in the Hassan district, within walking distance of the Hassan Tower and the Mausoleum of Mohammed V. It offers dormitory-style rooms with shared bathrooms, as well as private rooms with ensuite bathrooms.

Day 3: Chefchaouen

For breakfast, head to Café Maure, located inside the Kasbah of the Udayas. This café offers a panoramic view of the river Bouregreg and the Atlantic Ocean and serves traditional Moroccan tea, coffee, and pastries.

Take an early morning bus or taxi from Rabat to Chefchaouena, a picturesque blue city in the Rif Mountains (approx. 4 hours journey). Check in at your hotel and freshen up.

Upon arrival, take a stroll around the charming blue-washed streets of the medina and admire the unique architecture and colorful tiles.

Visit the Kasbah Museum, a former fortress that now houses a collection of local artifacts and exhibits on the history of Chefchaouen and the surrounding region.

For lunch, head to Casa Aladdin, a restaurant located inside the Kasbah, and try some traditional Moroccan tagine again or couscous.

After lunch, hike to the Spanish Mosque, located on a hilltop outside of the medina, and enjoy the panoramic views of Chefchaouen and the surrounding mountains.

Visit the Ras El-Maa waterfall, located just outside the medina, and enjoy the peaceful scenery.

For dinner, head to Bab Ssour, a restaurant located in the medina that offers traditional Moroccan cuisine with a twist.

After dinner, you can explore the nightlife of Chefchaouen. Head to one of the rooftop bars in the medina, such as Casa Perleta or Bar de la Kasbah, and enjoy a drink while admiring the stunning views of the blue-washed city.

Where to stay:

For your stay in Chefchaouen, we recommend Hotel Dar Zman, a charming traditional Moroccan guesthouse located in the heart of the medina that offers comfortable rooms and excellent amenities.

Day 4: Fes

Stay your day with a healthy breakfast. Head to Café Aladdin, located in the heart of the medina, and try some traditional Moroccan pastries and coffee.

Take an early morning bus or taxi from Chefchaouen to Fes, one of the oldest and largest medieval cities in the world (approx. 4 hours journey). Check in at your hotel and freshen up.

Upon arrival and freshening up if needed, head to the Al-Attarine Madrasa, a beautiful Islamic school built in the 14th century. Admire the intricate tile work and calligraphy, and imagine what it would have been like to study here centuries ago.

After that, head to the nearby Chouara Tannery, one of the largest and oldest tanneries in Fes, where you can see leather being dyed and treated in traditional vats.

For lunch, order a plate of tajine, a classic Moroccan dish made with meat, vegetables, and spices. There are many great tajine restaurants in Fes, but make sure to try one that uses a traditional earthenware pot for cooking.

After lunch, visit the Bab Bou Jeloud gate, an iconic entrance to the medina that features stunning blue and green tile work.

Explore the streets of the medina and visit the many souks (markets) that offer a variety of goods such as spices, textiles, and pottery.

For dinner, head to Café Clock once again and try some of their famous camel burgers or vegetarian options.

After dinner, you can head to Dar Batha, a former palace that now houses a museum of traditional Moroccan arts and crafts.

Alternatively, you can experience the vibrant nightlife of Fes by heading to one of the many bars and clubs in the city.

Where to stay:

For your stay in Fes, I recommend Riad Laaroussa, a beautiful traditional Moroccan guesthouse located in the heart of the medina that offers comfortable rooms and excellent amenities.

Day 5: Fes

For breakfast, head to Café Clock, a popular café in the medina that serves traditional Moroccan breakfast dishes such as Chickpea Stew and harira soup.

Start your day by visiting the University of Al Quaraouiyine, founded in 859 AD and considered to be the oldest continuously operating university in the world.

Visit the Royal Palace of Fes, a stunning complex of palaces, gardens, and mosques that showcases the city's rich history and architecture.

For Lunch, head to the Ruined Garden, a restaurant with a beautiful garden that serves Moroccan and Mediterranean cuisine.

After Lunch, Head to the Mellah, Fes' Jewish quarter, to explore the charming streets and architecture of this historic neighborhood.

Head to the Jardin Jnan Sbil, a beautiful public garden in the heart of Fes that offers a peaceful oasis from the hustle and bustle of the city.

For dinner, head to Restaurant L'Ambre, a highly-rated restaurant in the medina that offers traditional Moroccan cuisine with a modern twist.

After dinner, head to one of the many rooftop bars or cafes in the city, such as Café Clock or Café Fez, and enjoy a cup of Moroccan mint tea while taking in the stunning views of the city at night.

Where to stay:

For your second night in Fes, you may choose to stay at the same accommodation as the night before, Riad Laaroussa, or switch to another option such as Dar Seffarine, a beautifully restored 14th-century guesthouse located in the heart of the medina.

Day 6: Sahara Desert

Start your day early and head south towards the town of Erfoud, which is often used as a base for exploring the Sahara desert.

Along the way, you'll pass through the stunning Ziz Valley, a beautiful oasis that's home to thousands of palm trees.

For breakfast, stop at a local café or restaurant in one of the towns along the way and try some traditional Moroccan pancakes called "baghrir" with some honey.

Once you arrive in Erfoud, meet your guide and head out into the Sahara desert.

Explore the stunning desert landscape, including towering dunes, rocky outcroppings, and vast stretches of desert wilderness.

Take a camel ride into the heart of the desert and experience the traditional way of travel in this region.

For lunch, stop for a picnic in the desert and enjoy some traditional Moroccan dishes such as couscous and tagine cooked over an open fire.

As the sun begins to set, find a good spot to watch the sunset over the desert dunes. This is a truly unforgettable experience that you won't want to miss!

After the sun sets, head back to your campsite and enjoy a traditional Moroccan dinner under the stars.

Listen to traditional music and enjoy a cup of mint tea around the campfire, or take a guided night walk to learn more about the desert and its unique ecosystem.

Spend the night in a traditional Berber camp, complete with comfortable tents, warm blankets, and all the amenities you need for a comfortable night's sleep.

Fall asleep to the sounds of the desert and wake up early to catch the sunrise over the dunes.

Where to stay:

There are a variety of options for overnight stays in the Sahara desert, ranging from basic campsites to luxury desert lodges. Some popular options include Erg Chebbi Luxury Desert Camp, Merzouga Luxury Desert Camp, and Sahara Luxury Camp.

Day 7: Ouarzazate

On the seventh day of your trip, head out to Ouarzazate, a city in the Atlas Mountains that is known as the "door of the desert"

Begin your day with breakfast at your accommodation in Ouarzazate. Try some traditional Moroccan pancakes or bread with honey and mint tea.

Check-in at your hotel in Ouarzazate.

After freshening up, Head out to explore the Kasbah of Taourirt, a UNESCO World Heritage Site and one of the most impressive fortified villages in the region.

Take a guided tour of the Kasbah and learn about its fascinating history and architecture.

After visiting the Kasbah of Taourirt, head to the Atlas Film Studios, located just outside Ouarzazate. This is one of the largest film studios in the world and has been used as a location for many famous movies and TV shows, including Gladiator, Lawrence of Arabia, and Game of Thrones.

For lunch, head to Restaurant La Kasbah des Sables, a restaurant that serves traditional Moroccan cuisine with a modern twist.

After Lunch, visit the Atlas Film Studios, which has been the setting for many Hollywood films. Take a tour of the studios and see the sets and props used in some of your favorite movies.

As the sun begins to set, head to the Ait Benhaddou Kasbah, another UNESCO World Heritage Site and one of the most famous kasbahs in Morocco.

Take a guided tour of the kasbah and learn about its history and significance. Make sure to climb to the top of the kasbah for incredible views of the surrounding landscape.

For dinner, head to a local restaurant and try some traditional Moroccan dishes such as harira soup, pastilla, or kebabs.

Spend the night in a traditional Moroccan riad in Ouarzazate. Riads are traditional Moroccan houses with a central courtyard or garden, often converted into small hotels or guesthouses. Enjoy the unique architecture and decor of your riad and relax after a long day of sightseeing.

Where to stay:

There are many options for accommodation in Ouarzazate, including luxury hotels, budget hotels, and traditional riads. Some popular options include Le Berbere Palace, Le Temple des Arts, and Riad Ouarzazate.

Day 8: Marrakech

Begin your day with breakfast at your accommodation in Ouarzazate. Try some traditional Moroccan pancakes or bread with honey and mint tea.

Take the bus to Marrakech, a bustling city with a vibrant market. Check-in at your hotel in Marrakech.

Upon arrival, visit the Bahia Palace, a beautiful palace with gardens and fountains.

For lunch, head to Cafe Arabe, a popular rooftop restaurant that serves Moroccan and Mediterranean cuisine.

After lunch, head to the Bahia Palace, a 19th-century palace with beautiful gardens and intricate architecture. Take a guided tour of the palace and learn about its history and significance.

Next, head to the vibrant and bustling Jemaa el-Fnaa square, where you can see snake charmers, street performers, and food vendors selling delicious Moroccan snacks.

As the sun begins to set, head to the Koutoubia Mosque, the largest mosque in Marrakech. Admire the beautiful architecture and hear the call to prayer.

For dinner, head to a local restaurant and try some traditional Moroccan dishes such as harira soup, pastilla, or kebabs.

After dinner, head to one of Marrakech's many rooftop bars and enjoy a drink with a view of the city.

Spend the night in a traditional Moroccan riad in Marrakech. Riads are traditional Moroccan houses with a central courtyard or garden, often converted into small hotels or guesthouses. Enjoy the unique architecture and decor of your riad and relax after a long day of sightseeing.

Where to stay:

There are many options for accommodation in Marrakech, including luxury hotels, budget hotels, and traditional riads. Some popular options include La Maison Arabe, Riad Be Marrakech, and Riad Jona.

Day 9: Marrakech

Marrakech is a city that's full of surprises, and there's always something new to discover. On your second day in the city, explore some of Marrakech's lesser-known attractions and hidden gems.

Start your day with a leisurely breakfast at Cafe Clock, a cozy cafe that's known for its delicious breakfast dishes. Order the shakshuka, a flavorful egg dish that's popular in North Africa and the Middle East, along with a cup of strong Moroccan coffee.

After breakfast, head to the Maison de la Photographie, a small museum that showcases vintage photographs of Morocco. The museum is housed in a beautifully restored 19th-century riad, and the photographs offer a fascinating glimpse into Morocco's past.

For lunch, head to the trendy Gueliz neighborhood, which is home to several hip cafes and restaurants. Check out Cafe du Livre, a bookshop cafe that serves up delicious sandwiches, salads, and pastries.

After lunch, take a stroll through the nearby Majorelle Garden, a beautiful oasis that's filled with exotic plants and vibrant colors.

In the afternoon, visit the Ben Youssef Madrasa, a stunning Islamic college that was built in the 14th century. The madrasa features intricate tilework, carved woodwork, and a tranquil courtyard that's perfect for escaping the bustle of the city.

For dinner, head to Nomad, a stylish restaurant that offers a modern take on traditional Moroccan cuisine. Try the harira soup, a hearty and flavorful soup that's often eaten during Ramadan, and the lamb tagine with prunes and almonds.

After dinner, head to the rooftop terrace at Cafe Arabe, where you can enjoy a cocktail and take in the stunning views of the city at night.

Where to stay:

For your second night in Marrakech, consider staying at La Maison Arabe, a luxurious riad that's located in the heart of the medina. The riad features beautiful Moroccan decor, a swimming pool, and a spa, and it's the perfect place to relax after a day of exploring the city.

Rest well and enjoy your final day in Marrakech before your adventure in Morocco comes to a close.

Day 10: Departure

On your last day in Morocco, it's time to say goodbye to this beautiful country. Enjoy your last breakfast in Morocco before checking out of your hotel.

Start your day with a traditional Moroccan breakfast of Msemen (a type of flatbread) and honey, along with some fresh fruit and a cup of mint tea. You can find many breakfast places near your accommodation.

After breakfast, pack your bags and check out of your accommodation. If you have some time before your flight, you can take a walk around the neighborhood or do some last-minute shopping for souvenirs.

For lunch, try a plate of couscous, a classic Moroccan dish made with semolina and vegetables, and sometimes meat. It's a filling and delicious meal, and you can find it in many restaurants throughout the city.

After lunch, head to the airport or train station for your departure. If you have some extra time, you can visit a nearby museum or attraction before leaving.

Depart from Marrakech for your next destination.

I hope this itinerary helps you plan your trip to Morocco! It is important to note that Morocco is a diverse and complex country with many different regions and cultures, so this itinerary is just one possible way to experience the country. It is always a good idea to research and plan to make the most of your trip.

Nightlife in Morocco

Morocco has a vibrant and varied nightlife scene, especially in its major cities like Casablanca, Marrakech, and Tangier. Here are some of the things you can expect:

1. Nightclubs and bars:

You can find a variety of nightclubs and bars in Morocco's cities, offering a mix of music styles and drinks.

2. Live music and entertainment:

Many venues in Morocco offer live music and entertainment, ranging from traditional Moroccan music to international acts.

3. Night markets:

In some cities, you can find night markets where vendors sell food, drinks, and other goods. These can be fun and lively places to spend an evening.

4. Cafes and restaurants:

Many cafes and restaurants in Morocco stay open late into the night, offering a relaxing place to socialize and enjoy some food and drinks.

It's worth noting that Morocco is a predominantly Muslim country, so the nightlife scene may be more subdued than in some other countries. Additionally, alcohol consumption is not as common or widely accepted as it is in some other places. However, there are still plenty of options for those looking to enjoy the nightlife in Morocco.

Morocco Facts, Culture, Traditions.

Morocco is a nation situated in North Africa, bordering the Atlantic Ocean and the Mediterranean Sea. Here are some facts, culture, and customs of Morocco:

1. Facts:

- Morocco has a population of around 36 million people.

- Arabic and Berber are the official languages of Morocco, however, French is widely spoken.

- The currency of Morocco is the Moroccan dirham.

- The capital of Morocco is Rabat, while the biggest city is Casablanca.
- Morocco is recognized for its colorful culture, magnificent beaches, and breathtaking architecture.

- Morocco is the world's biggest exporter of phosphates.

2. Culture:

- Morocco's culture is a combination of Arab, Berber, and European influences.

- Islam is the prevalent religion of Morocco, with almost 99% of the people being Muslim.

- Family is a fundamental component of Moroccan society, and hospitality is highly appreciated.

- Moroccan cuisine is recognized for its spices and tastes, such as cumin, paprika, and saffron. Tagine and couscous are two typical Moroccan foods.

- Moroccan music encompasses traditional Berber and Arab traditions, as well as current pop and hip-hop.

3. Traditions:

- Ramadan is an important religious occasion in Morocco, and many people fast throughout the day and break their fast with a meal called iftar at dusk.

- Eid al-Fitr is a three-day celebration that commemorates the end of Ramadan and is celebrated with eating and gift-giving.

- The Moroccan wedding ceremony is a multi-day affair that features traditional music, dancing, and cuisine.

- Henna is a traditional custom in Morocco, commonly used for decorating the hands and feet at special events.

- Moroccan carpets and textiles are known for their beautiful patterns and are regularly utilized in traditional rites and festivals.

Moroccan Local Cuisine

Moroccan cuisine is noted for its bright tastes, spices, and ingredients. Here are some classic Moroccan foods you may wish to try:

1. Tagine:

A substantial stew composed of meat (typically lamb, beef, or chicken), veggies, and spices, cooked in a cone-shaped clay pot. There are several types of tagine, including tagine with prunes, tagine with olives, and tagine with preserved lemons.

2. Couscous:

A classic meal in Morocco prepared from semolina grain generally served with meat, vegetables, and a delicious broth. Couscous is frequently called the national dish of Morocco.

3. Harira:

A classic soup often consumed during Ramadan, prepared with tomatoes, chickpeas, lentils, and a variety of spices. It is commonly served with dates and other dry fruits.

4. Pastilla:

A savory pie prepared with chicken or pigeon, almonds, and spices, wrapped in phyllo dough and coated with powdered sugar and cinnamon.

5. Mechoui:

An entire roasted lamb or sheep, seasoned with spices and slow-cooked till soft and fragrant.

6. Kefta tagine:

Meatballs prepared with ground beef or lamb, combined with spices and onions, then cooked in a tomato-based sauce. It is commonly served with eggs.

7. Zaalouk:

A tasty salad prepared with eggplant and tomatoes, seasoned with garlic, cumin, and paprika.

8. B'stilla:

A sweet and savory pastry composed of layers of phyllo dough, ground pigeon or chicken, and almonds, seasoned with cinnamon and sugar.

9. Sardines:

Morocco is noted for its fresh sardines, generally grilled or fried and served with a side of lemon and herbs.

10.   Khobz:

Traditional Moroccan bread is traditionally offered with every meal.

These are just a handful of the numerous amazing cuisines you may enjoy in Morocco. Be sure to also taste some of the country's famed drinks and sweets, including mint tea and baklava.

Morocco's Top Hotels

Morocco boasts numerous magnificent and top-rated hotels that provide outstanding service, facilities, and stunning views. Here are some of the best hotels in Morocco:

1. La Mamounia, Marrakech:

La Mamounia is a premium hotel situated in Marrakech, Morocco. It was initially erected in 1923 and has had various restorations and improvements since then. The hotel is nestled in a lovely 17-acre garden with views of the Atlas Mountains.

La Mamounia is noted for its exquisite décor, comprising authentic Moroccan architecture, delicate tile work, and sumptuous furniture. The hotel provides a range of amenities, including rooms, suites, and private riads (traditional Moroccan dwellings).

In addition to its gorgeous lodgings, La Mamounia provides several facilities and activities for visitors to enjoy, including a spa, fitness center, tennis courts, and various restaurants and bars. The hotel also boasts a magnificent outdoor pool surrounded by lush flora and a poolside bar.

La Mamounia is situated within a short distance from Marrakech's famed medina, a UNESCO World Heritage Site. Guests may explore the busy souks (markets), visit ancient monuments like the Bahia Palace and the Koutoubia Mosque, or just absorb the city's colorful culture and nightlife.

Overall, La Mamounia is a luxury and wonderful resort for visitors wishing to experience the beauty and warmth of Morocco.

2. Royal Mansour, Marrakech:

The Royal Mansour is a premium hotel situated in the center of Marrakech, Morocco. It is supposed to seem like a typical Moroccan castle, with delicate tile work, towering arches, and gorgeous courtyards.

The hotel was commissioned by King Mohammed VI of Morocco and took over three years to complete. It has 53 individual riads (traditional Moroccan dwellings) that are spread out over five acres of grounds. Each riad is beautifully furnished and consists o a pool, patio, and courtyard.

The Royal Mansour also provides several services and activities for visitors, including a spa, fitness center, various restaurants and bars, and a gorgeous outdoor pool. The hotel's spa is especially remarkable since it provides a variety of traditional Moroccan therapies utilizing natural substances like argan oil and rose water.

Guests at the Royal Mansour may also enjoy a choice of cultural activities, such as cooking workshops, calligraphy lessons, and tours of Marrakech's ancient landmarks. The hotel is situated only a short distance from the city's famed medina, where visitors can explore the colorful souks (markets), visit ancient buildings like the Bahia Palace and the Koutoubia Mosque, and soak up the city's rich culture and history.

Overall, the Royal Mansour is a beautiful resort for visitors wishing to experience the beauty and warmth of Morocco in an opulent environment.

3. Mandarin Oriental, Marrakech:

Mandarin Oriental, Marrakech is a premium resort situated in the Palmeraie area of Marrakech, Morocco. The resort comprises 54 individual villas and 9 suites, each with a pool and beautiful garden. The villas and suites are constructed with a combination of modern and traditional Moroccan styles, with lofty ceilings, beautiful tilework, and rich carpets.

The resort provides a choice of eating alternatives, including the trademark Mes'Lalla restaurant which serves contemporary Moroccan cuisine, and the Pool Garden restaurant which offers light Mediterranean food. The resort also has a spa with a variety of treatments, a fitness center, and a tennis court.

In addition to its exquisite facilities, Mandarin Oriental, Marrakech is bordered by beautiful gardens and palm groves, creating a tranquil ambiance for guests. The resort is also situated near several of Marrakech's notable sites, including the Medina, the Bahia Palace, and the Majorelle Garden.

4. Kasbah Tamadot, Atlas Mountains:

Kasbah Tamadot is a magnificent mountain hideaway set in the foothills of the Atlas Mountains, near the hamlet of Asni in Morocco. The Kasbah is a spectacular hilltop stronghold that has been turned into a charming boutique hotel by Sir Richard Branson's Virgin Limited Edition.

The Kasbah includes 28 luxury rooms and suites, each distinctively designed with traditional Moroccan furniture and contemporary conveniences. The rooms provide amazing views of the surrounding mountains and valleys. The hotel also provides the option of private Berber Tents for a unique experience.

Guests may enjoy a multitude of activities throughout their stay, including trekking in the Atlas Mountains, visiting local Berber towns, or just resting by the outdoor infinity pool. The hotel also has a spa, a hammam, and a fitness center.

Dining at Kasbah Tamadot is a gourmet experience, with an emphasis on utilizing fresh, local foods. Guests may savor traditional Moroccan specialties as well as foreign cuisine in the Kanoun Restaurant, or have a private meal in one of the hotel's gorgeous locales, such as the rooftop terrace or the candle-lit Asmoun Lounge.

Kasbah Tamadot is a great place for people seeking a calm getaway in a stunning natural environment, with a touch of luxury and a cultural flair.

5. Sofitel Essaouira Mogador Golf & Spa, Essaouira:

Sofitel Essaouira Mogador Golf & Spa is a magnificent 5-star hotel situated in Essaouira, a seaside city in western Morocco. The hotel is located near the Mogador Golf Course, which provides visitors with beautiful views of the Atlantic Ocean and the surrounding countryside.

The hotel includes 147 large and attractively designed rooms and suites, each giving a delightful stay. Guests may pick from a range of accommodation categories, including Superior, Luxury, Prestige, and Opera Suites, all of which are equipped with contemporary amenities like air conditioning, free Wi-Fi, satellite TV, and a private bathroom.

The hotel also has a choice of eating alternatives, including Le Cafe Kasbah, which serves traditional Moroccan cuisine, L'Atlantique, a seafood restaurant with ocean views, and La Nasse, a bar situated by the pool. Guests may also enjoy a selection of recreational amenities, including an outdoor pool, a fitness center, and a spa providing a choice of services.

In addition to its exquisite facilities, the hotel's location offers it a perfect base for visiting the lovely city of Essaouira, noted for its gorgeous medina, vibrant markets, and breathtaking port. The hotel is only a short drive from the city center, where visitors may enjoy the city's rich history and cultural legacy.

6. La Sultana Oualidia, Oualidia:

La Sultana Oualidia is a magnificent boutique hotel situated in the lovely seaside town of Oualidia, Morocco. The hotel is located on a private beach facing the Atlantic Ocean and is surrounded by magnificent gardens and lagoons.

The hotel includes 12 beautifully themed rooms and suites, each giving a distinctive and enjoyable experience. The rooms are meant to merge traditional Moroccan flair with contemporary comforts, like air conditioning, free Wi-Fi, and a private bathroom with a bathtub or shower. Some rooms additionally offer a balcony or patio with ocean views.

Guests may enjoy several eating options at the hotel, including La Table de la Sultana, which provides a combination of Moroccan and international cuisine cooked with fresh, locally sourced ingredients. The hotel also offers a bar and lounge area, where guests may relax with a drink and enjoy the wonderful views of the ocean.

The hotel provides several recreational amenities, including a heated outdoor pool, a spa providing a choice of treatments, and a private beach where guests may enjoy swimming and sunbathing. The hotel also provides many activities, including kayaking, fishing, and bird viewing in the neighboring lagoons.

In addition to its exquisite facilities, the hotel's location gives it a great base for visiting the town of Oualidia, noted for its gorgeous beaches, calm lagoons, and wonderful seafood. The hotel is only a short walk from the town center, where visitors can experience local markets, cafés, and restaurants.

7. Riad Fes, Fes:

Riad Fes is a beautiful boutique hotel situated in the center of the old city of Fes, Morocco. The hotel is built in a renovated 17th-century palace and has authentic Moroccan architecture and design.

The hotel provides 30 distinctively furnished rooms and suites, each boasting a combination of traditional Moroccan décor with contemporary conveniences such as air conditioning, free Wi-Fi, and a private bathroom with a bathtub or shower. Some rooms additionally offer a private balcony or patio with views of the city or the hotel's grounds.

Guests may enjoy several eating options at the hotel, including the L'Ambre restaurant, which provides a mix of Moroccan and international cuisine, and the Rooftop Terrace, where guests can have a drink while taking in the spectacular views of the city. The hotel also has a lounge and bar area, where guests may relax with a drink and chat with other guests.

The hotel provides some recreational amenities, including a heated indoor pool, a hammam, and a spa providing a choice of treatments. The hotel also provides several activities, including guided tours of the city, culinary workshops, and traditional Moroccan music and dance performances.

In addition to its exquisite facilities, the hotel's location offers it a perfect base for visiting the historic city of Fes, noted for its rich history, lively culture, and gorgeous architecture. The hotel is situated within walking distance of the city's principal attractions, including the ancient medina, the Royal Palace, and the Bou Inania Madrasa.

Top Beaches in Morocco

Morocco is recognized for its magnificent beaches that are great for relaxation, swimming, and water sports. Here are some of the greatest beaches in Morocco:

1. Essaouira Beach:

Essaouira Beach is a magnificent beach located in the coastal town of Essaouira, which is situated on the Atlantic coast of Morocco. The beach is recognized for its long length of golden sand, crystal blue seas, and high winds, which make it a popular place for windsurfing and kite surfing.

Aside from water sports, Essaouira Beach is also an excellent area for swimming, sunbathing, and resting. There are many beachside cafés and restaurants where you can have a wonderful meal or a refreshing drink while taking in the lovely ocean views.

In addition to its natural beauty, Essaouira is also noted for its picturesque ancient town, which is a UNESCO World Heritage Site. The village is dotted with small lanes, historic blue and white houses, and vibrant marketplaces offering anything from spices to homemade goods.

Overall, Essaouira Beach is a must-visit place for anybody visiting Morocco, whether you're wanting to relax on the beach or explore the town's rich culture and history.

2. **Agadir Beach:**

Agadir Beach is a prominent tourist resort situated in the city of Agadir, Morocco. It is famed for its lengthy stretch of golden sand that spans roughly 10 kilometers along the

Atlantic coast. The beach is large and expansive, allowing lots of area for sunbathing and swimming.

The waves at Agadir Beach are very quiet and safe for swimming, making it a perfect site for families with children. The beach is also popular with surfers, offering waves that are suited for beginners and expert surfers alike.

In addition to sunbathing and swimming, visitors to Agadir Beach may enjoy a choice of sports such as jet skiing, parasailing, and camel rides. There is also a selection of seaside cafés, restaurants, and pubs where guests may relax and enjoy the views.

Overall, Agadir Beach is a lovely and dynamic place that provides something for everyone, whether you're searching for a calm beach holiday or an energetic adventure.

3. Legzira Beach:

Legzira Beach is a lovely and unusual beach situated on the Atlantic coast of Morocco, near the town of Sidi Ifni. It is recognized for its spectacular red sandstone arches that rise from the sand and water, forming a natural tunnel-like structure. These arches were sculpted by erosion over thousands of years and are a major draw for visitors and photographers.

In addition to the arches, Legzira Beach is particularly famed for its broad stretch of sand and gorgeous blue seas. It is an excellent area for swimming, sunbathing, and exploring the neighboring cliffs and caves. The beach is rather remote, offering it a calm and pleasant respite from the throng of some of Morocco's more famous tourist spots.

However, it's worth mentioning that owing to its position and the powerful waves of the Atlantic, Legzira Beach might be unsafe for swimming during certain times of the year. Visitors should always exercise care and heed any posted warnings or advice from local authorities.

4. Asilah Beach:

Asilah Beach is a magnificent and attractive beach situated in the little town of Asilah on the northern coast of Morocco. It is famed for its silky white sand, crystal-clear seas, and magnificent views of the Atlantic Ocean. The beach is a popular location for visitors and residents alike, providing a variety of activities such as swimming, sunbathing, and water sports.

In addition to its natural beauty, Asilah Beach is also recognized for its lovely village, which is rich with classic Moroccan buildings and vivid paintings. The town is noted for its cultural festivals, such as the Asilah Arts Festival, which presents a range of artistic and cultural activities during the summer months.

Visitors to Asilah Beach may also enjoy visiting the neighboring medieval medina, which boasts narrow lanes, ancient walls, and a variety of stores and restaurants offering authentic Moroccan items and food. Overall, Asilah Beach is a must-visit site for everyone searching for a pleasant and culturally interesting beach experience in Morocco.

5. **El Jadida Beach:**

El Jadida Beach is a prominent tourist site situated in the city of El Jadida, which is a coastal city in western Morocco. The beach is noted for its long length of golden sand and crystal blue seas, which make it a fantastic site for swimming, sunbathing, and water sports.

El Jadida Beach is also recognized for its gorgeous vistas and scenic surroundings. The beach is backed by cliffs and hills covered in lush foliage, and there are numerous cafés and restaurants along the promenade where guests may enjoy a meal or a drink while taking in the wonderful views.

In addition to its natural beauty, El Jadida Beach is also noted for its historical importance. The city of El Jadida was created by the Portuguese in the 16th century, and many of the city's historic sites, such as the Portuguese Cistern and the Portuguese Fortified City of Mazagan, are situated near the shore.

Overall, El Jadida Beach is a must-visit place for anybody visiting Morocco, whether they are interested in history, culture, or just spending a day at the beach.

6. Tifnit Beach:

Tifnit Beach is a lovely beach situated on the Atlantic coast of Morocco, near the town of Tifnit. It is noted for its pure seas, golden beaches, and gorgeous surroundings. The beach is relatively private, making it a fantastic site for people wishing to escape the throng and enjoy some peace & quiet.

One of the distinctive attractions of Tifnit Beach is the existence of a small fishing hamlet nearby, which allows tourists the chance to experience the traditional way of life of the local fisherman. The area is home to a few modest cafés and restaurants, where you may enjoy some great seafood delicacies.

Tifnit Beach is also a popular site for surfing, especially during the winter months when the waves are at their greatest. However, the beach is not monitored by lifeguards, thus visitors should use care while swimming or surfing.

Overall, Tifnit Beach is a must-visit site for anybody visiting Morocco and searching for a tranquil and gorgeous beach experience.

7. Oualidia Beach:

Oualidia Beach is a magnificent length of shoreline situated in the little fishing community of Oualidia, Morocco. It is a popular spot for vacationers wanting a more laid-back and private beach experience.

One of the unusual aspects of Oualidia Beach is its lagoon, which is protected from the Atlantic Ocean by a thin strip of sand. The lagoon is a popular site for swimming, kayaking, and windsurfing since the calm waters make it simple to traverse.

In addition to the lagoon, Oualidia Beach provides spectacular views of the surrounding cliffs and slopes and is home to a variety of animals, including flamingos, egrets, and other bird species.

The beach is particularly well-known for its fresh seafood, which is gathered daily by local fishermen and served at the numerous restaurants and cafés that line the coastline.

Overall, Oualidia Beach is a must-visit site for anybody visiting Morocco who is searching for a tranquil and gorgeous beach experience.

These are just a handful of the greatest beaches in Morocco, but there are many more gorgeous sites to discover along the country's breathtaking coastline.

Conclusion

In conclusion, Morocco provides a unique and remarkable experience to every tourist seeking adventure, culture, and history. From the busy marketplaces of Marrakech to the tranquil beach village of Essaouira, Morocco is a nation full of contrasts and surprises.

Visitors may visit the historic towns of Fez and Meknes, trek in the Atlas Mountains, or relax on the magnificent beaches of Agadir. The local cuisine is a combination of Arab, Berber, and French influences, creating a rich and tasty gastronomic experience.

The people of Morocco are famed for their warmth and friendly demeanor, making guests feel at home. With its rich history, various landscapes, and lively culture, Morocco is undoubtedly a must-visit destination for every visitor.

Printed in Great Britain
by Amazon

25685573R00099